Goggleby Stone

Shap Abbey

2

Shap and Rosgill

"......... *the gaze of many centuries:*
now lost, save what we find on remnants huge
of stone, or marble swart; their import gone,
their wisdom long since fled."

John Keats

Shap village was once a much busier place in relation to its strategic position on the road we know as the A6, which for hundreds of years was the main route between North West England and Scotland. At its peak during the 1960s, before the motorway opened in 1970, over 9,000 vehicles came through the village every day.

monks chanting,
lino print for bronze panel

Shap's origins go back to Neolithic times, when there was almost certainly an avenue of standing stones here, perhaps 2.5 kilometres in length, forming a sweeping curve along what is now the western side of the village. With a few notable exceptions, most of the stones have long since been removed.

There were also two standing stone circles. The remains of one of these can be seen from the main road 2.5 kilometres south of Shap village, at the base of the railway embankment. Six huge boulders of Shap granite and several smaller stones are all that remain of what must have been a very impressive monument, destroyed when the railway was built in the middle of the 19th century.

The Goggleby stone is close to the footpath on the return route to Shap.

Goggleby stone

view towards the Lake District

Although the Shap area is now dominated on its eastern side by the motorway, there is a tranquil area to the west where a beautiful ancient landscape leads across to the Lake District.

Turn right out of the car park; go past the school and cross the road on the pedestrian crossing. Continue along the road past a small building with arches in its walls on your left.

This is the Market Cross, originally built with open archways as a shelter for the market when the village was granted its market charter, in 1687. The village archive is kept here now and is open every weekend between May and September and the first Saturday of every month in winter.

At the north end of the village, turn left onto the Bampton / Haweswater road. Go along the road until you turn right through double wooden gates, where there is a signpost indicating two footpaths - one to Shap Abbey and the other to Rosgill. Our route is the one to Rosgill. Keep straight on to the far side of the field and go through a gate which is out of sight, well to the right of the gate you can see from here.

Continue at the same angle to another gate and continue to the far corner of the next field.

If you look towards the farm buildings ahead, over to the right of the trees, you will see a large stone known as the Thunderstone. This is one of the few stones that have survived from the great Neolithic avenue at its northern end.

Go over the wall-stile out onto the lane.

> There are two more large stones lying in
> the corner of the next field which may also
> have been part of the avenue.

Turn right along the lane and then left over a wall-stile
signposted Public Footpath.

> You are now entering the Lake District
> National Park. The Lake District was one of
> the first National Parks to be designated,
> two years after the 1949 National Parks and
> Access to the Countryside Act. National
> Park status reflects the outstanding qualities
> of a particular landscape. But the title
> 'national park' is a misnomer, as they are
> not parks in an exclusively recreational
> sense, nor are they nationally owned. All
> the land is privately owned and access
> across farmland is confined to public rights
> of way.

> There is a well-preserved lime-kiln over to
> the right. The lumps and hollows in the field
> remain from a time when the limestone rock
> was excavated, packed into the kiln with
> layers of fuel and burned to produce lime
> dust for fertilising the fields.

Pass to the left of the lime-kiln over to the far corner
of the field, where the fence joins the wall. Cross a
step-stile into the next field and go straight on, keeping
the wall nearby on your left, and you will come to a tall
wall-stile with steps on both sides. This brings you into a
long, narrow field.

lime-kiln

Lake District looking towards Haweswater

The breathtaking view of the mountains ahead evokes a real sense of the Lake District's special National Park status. Haweswater is just visible in the middle. Originally it was a smaller natural lake, until the building of the dam in 1935 raised the water level by 29 metres, creating a reservoir six kilometres long and 600 metres wide. You may be lucky enough to see a golden eagle soaring over the valley around Haweswater, as it is the only place in England where they have been known to breed in recent times.

Although these eastern Lake District fells seem remote from the Eden valley they are, in fact, very much part of the river Eden's catchment landscape. Hundreds of becks flow down from them into the river Lowther which runs north to Brougham Castle, where it joins the river Eamont which, in turn, travels east from there and feeds into the river Eden south of Culgaith.

Continue to the far end of the field and cross another wall-stile. Walk round the right hand side of a grassy mound that covers the remains of another lime-kiln and keep bearing slightly left. Go through three more wall-stiles and then bear left to a pedestrian gate at the right hand end of a conifer plantation.

Rosgill

The river Lowther comes into view below
the woods and Rosgill village lies ahead,
surrounded by trees. Woodland is scarce
in east Cumbria so the trees around
Rosgill and along the river provide a very
valuable habitat for a variety of wildlife.
If you haven't seen an eagle, then you
will almost certainly see a buzzard gliding
above the woods between here and
Shap Abbey. Buzzards are known as
'tourists eagles' in Scotland, as they can be
mistaken for eagles although they are half
the size. Other birds of prey you may see
include kestrels, sparrow hawks and, very
occasionally late into the evening, tawny
and barn owls.

buzzard feeding on rabbit carcass
illustration based on © image Mike Lane (rspb-images.com)

13

Farming in Cumbria

Agriculture in Cumbria is mainly based on livestock eating grass. The region has been synonymous with rearing sheep since the early medieval period and at one time their wool was a vital part of its economy. Currently, however, fleeces are almost worthless and the hardy hill breeds of sheep, the Herdwick, Rough Fell and Swaledale, are much more valued as breeding stock and for the exceptional quality of their meat.

Cattle, too, have always been important in Cumbria. Kept originally as dual purpose animals, supplying local markets with both meat and milk, modern demands for increased productivity nationally have forced farmers to choose between keeping beef or dairy herds. Since 1990, over seven hundred dairy farms have disappeared from Cumbria and there are many more farmers specialising in beef.

But farmers in Cumbria today are also important as custodians of the landscape. The much loved pattern of enclosed fields in the valleys, the 'intake' land on the lower slopes and the vast expanse of the open fells is the culmination of centuries of grazing sheep and cattle. It is this grazed landscape which attracts the tourists and is probably now one of Cumbria's greatest economic assets.

looking towards Rosgill

Go through the gate, down the sloping field, through a wooden field gate and bear right. Cross two narrow fields over wall-stiles, then through a pedestrian gate into a small garden between two houses, where a wall-stile and steps bring you out onto the lane. Turn left down the lane to the bottom of the village.

Cross the bridge over the river Lowther and turn left through a wicket gate, along the track which curves right through a field gate. Turn immediately left. Do not walk up the obvious track, but follow the trod with the wall alongside on your left and the steep grassy bank on your right. Traverse the wall-stile and continue straight on, with the wall and then a fence on your left and a rocky outcrop over to the right. This is Fairy Crag.

> *"Once....once upon a time...*
> *like a dream you dream in the night,*
> *fairies and gnomes stole out*
> *in the leaf green light."*
>
> Walter de la Mare

fairies, lino print for bronze panel

The beck is Swindale Beck which runs down from the fells just south east of Haweswater and joins the river Lowther at Rosgill. Could the name 'Fairy Crag' originate from a local belief in fairies? Old Westmorland has a strong tradition of fairy mythology in relation to water. Apparently, fairies have a particular love of fast flowing streams and it is said that stone footbridges over mountain becks, when certain conditions prevail, are good places to see them.

Go over the beck on the stone packhorse bridge. Bear left up the slope on the other side and then keep straight ahead across the middle of this big field, to the wall corner opposite. Cross over the wall-stile into a paddock with a derelict building on your left. Go out of the paddock through the field gate ahead and bear left onto a tarmac surfaced track. Proceed along here for a short distance, turn left through a wooden field gate, cross the field, go through a gated wall-stile and then bear slightly right, across a grassy earth bank.

packhorse bridge

Shap Abbey

The earth bank and ditch extend south of here, then east to Shap Abbey and were probably field boundaries relating to the Abbey in Medieval times.

Keep straight on towards the telegraph pole over to the left of the wall corner. Keep just left of the telegraph pole, then bear gently down to the right, where you cross the small beck which flows into the main river which you can see again on your left.

The tower of Shap Abbey comes into view with the chimneys of Shap Fell limestone works beyond where limestone is processed - on a very different scale to the humble limekilns - for use in steel production.

Shap Abbey was built by a group of monks, known as the 'white canons' because they wore white robes woven from un-dyed sheep's fleeces. Originating from the Premonstratensian order of monks in northern France, they moved to Shap in the 13th century. Local landowners gave them land and donations in return for the promise of a guaranteed place in heaven. Despite their vows of austerity and poverty, they became relatively wealthy, surrounded by a supportive community of shepherds, gardeners and millers and an extensive and productive estate.

The monks dedicated the Abbey and the surrounding valley to God and Mary Magdalene who, in the Middle Ages, was the patron saint of mistresses.

Cross the ladder-stile and continue on to where the path skirts round to the right at the top of a steep bank overlooking the river. Go over another ladder-stile and carry straight on to the Abbey.

> The tower was built in the 16th century and the remains of other buildings, including a church, cloister, chapter house and refectory, are 13th century. North and south of the abbey there are also the remains of a water-mill, mill-race and fish-ponds.
>
> Interpretation panels on the site provide more details.

When you leave the Abbey, go out the same way you came in. The surfaced farm track and bridge to the right are private. Our route follows the path back along the track you came down to from the ladder-stile, but, instead of going back up to the ladder-stile, keep on the track and bear right through a field gate and over the river on the pedestrian bridge.

> Just past the gate, before you go over the bridge, you will see a narrow, walled track going off to the left, along which sheep were once driven and plunged into the river to wash their fleeces.

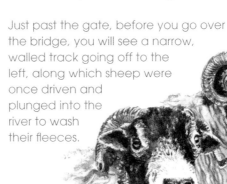

Swaledale sheep

bridge over river Lowther near Shap Abbey

Follow the track past the timber bungalow on your left
and go straight up the rough bank from the point where
the main track goes off to the left. A way-marker post at
the top of the bank shows the way. Turn right at the top
of the bank, go over a wall-stile beside a field gate and
continue alongside the fence on your right, where the
footpath follows the top side of Shap Abbey Woods.

The derelict wall on the other side of the fence is probably as old as the Abbey and provides the right conditions for slow-growing mosses, liverworts, lichen and ferns.

Cross another wall-stile, bear left and keep the wall on your left until you turn left over a stepped stile, which takes you to the other side of the wall where you turn right. Continue, with the wall on your right, to the wall's corner. Keep straight over to the corner of the next field and follow the wall to a wooden step-stile, past a house, out onto the lane at the top end of Keld.

Keld Chapel

ferns

Our route turns left here, but you may wish to visit the tiny chapel in Keld, which is just down towards the village on the left hand side.

Keld Chapel was apparently built, at sometime after 1350, by the monks of Shap Abbey, as a Chantry (for chanting mass). During the late 17th century it became a private house. It was given to the National Trust in 1917 after which it was restored as a chapel. A key is available from the house opposite.

Continue up the lane away from Keld and take a right turn over a wall-stile, into a field where you turn immediately left and follow the path along the side of the field, parallel with the lane. Cross a wall-stile into a second field. Just past this stile there is another wall-stile from the lane into the field, with a signpost indicating two paths to Shap. Ignore the one to the right and keep straight on. Go through two more wall-stiles, cross a walled track though a wall-stile on the other side, and carry on alongside the wall on your left.

The large standing stone is the Goggleby Stone, another survivor from the great Neolithic avenue. For many years it lay on its side, but was re-erected by the County Archaeologist in 1975. Excavation revealed it had been set in clay and wedged upright with stones packed around its base. Another of the avenue stones can be seen lying in the field over to the left.

Go over a wall-stile, along a short section of path fenced off from a tree plantation on your right, and over another wall-stile which brings you into a long, narrow field with a wall on your right. At the top of this slope, Shap village comes into view. Go through a pedestrian gate and along a short length of walled track between some houses, then through a field gate onto a back lane. Turn left and then right to the main road.

Turn right along the main road to the zebra crossing back to the car park to conclude your walk.

avenue of stones,
lino print for bronze panel